ROBOTS HELPING HUMANS

Natasha Vizcarra

Children's Press®
An imprint of Scholastic Inc.

Thank you to our expert content consultant:
Matthew VanCleave
Staff Engineer
Robotics Center
Stanford University

and our educational consultant:
Jackie Fego
Science Liaison
C.V. Starr Intermediate School
Brewster, NY

Library of Congress Cataloging-in-Publication Data available

ISBN 978-1-5461-7847-7 (library binding) | ISBN 978-1-5461-7848-4 (paperback) |
ISBN 978-1-5461-7849-1 (ebook)

10 9 8 7 6 5 4 3 2 1 26 27 28 29 30

Printed in China 62
First edition, 2026

Design by Kathleen Petelinsek
Series produced by Spooky Cheetah Press

Find the Truth!

Everything you are about to read is true ***except*** for one of the sentences on this page.

Which one is **TRUE**?

TRUE or FALSE Scientists have sent robots inside volcanoes.

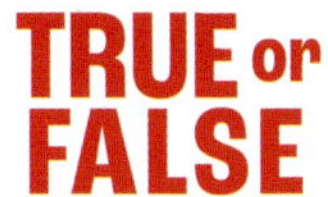

TRUE or FALSE Robots cannot work in teams.

Find the answers in this book.

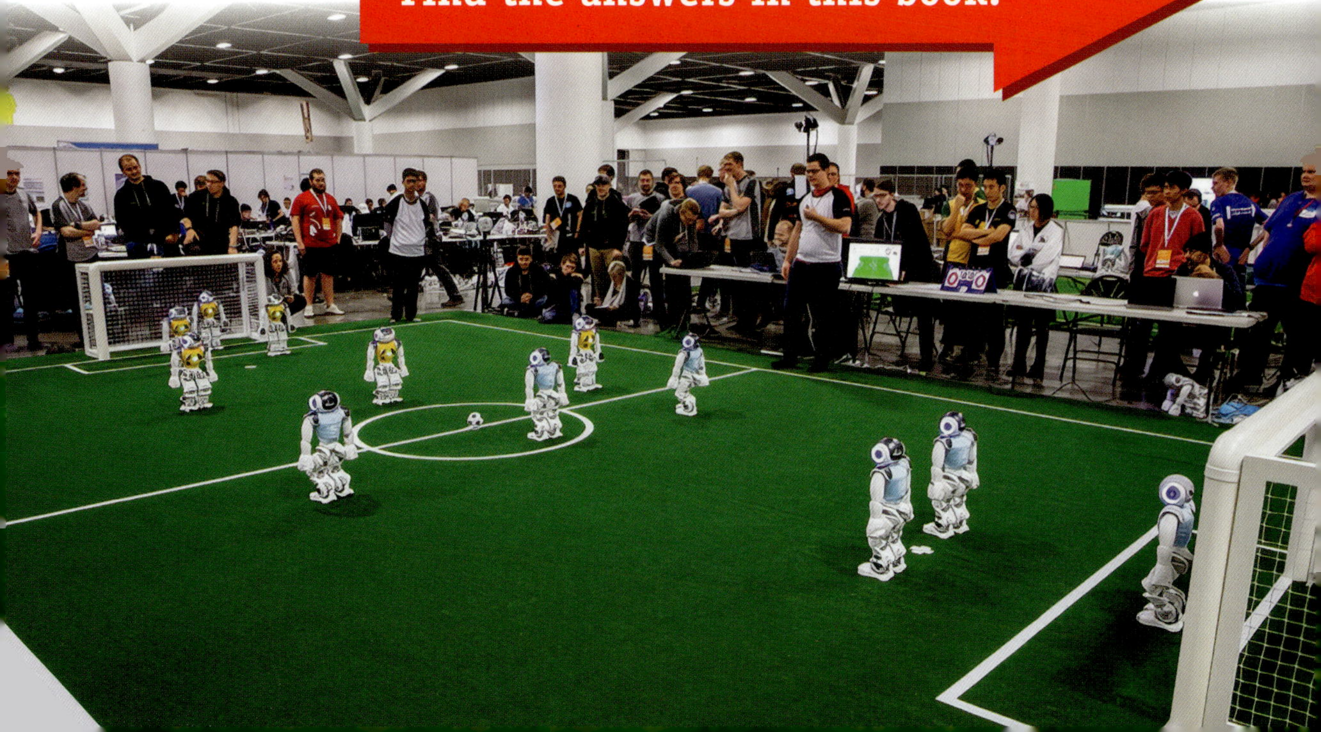

What's in This Book?

NASA's Dante II robot explores extreme environments.

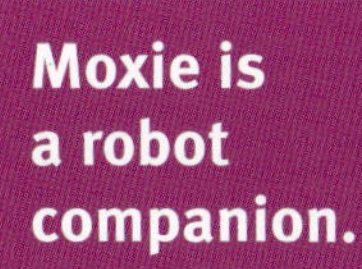

The BIG Truth

Does this look like a robot to you?

See what the kitten is sitting on? It is a **robot that can clean** your floor. That car that is parked on the street is also a robot. It is a **driverless taxi**. And that robot buzzing through the sewer pipe is cleaning away **toxic** chemicals.

You may not realize it, but many robots are around us and **make our lives easier and safer**. Yucky jobs, dangerous jobs, and boring jobs? They can handle those. **Jobs impossible for humans** to do by themselves? Tasks requiring extreme **precision**? Sign them up!

The Roomba is a robot vacum. Its inventor, Joe Jones, first called it the Dust Puppy.

Robot vacuums like this one are found in millions of homes worldwide.

Robots are machines capable of carrying out a **complex series of actions** automatically. Some robots look a bit like people. Some look like pets or other animals. Others look like machines. But all robots usually have **five main parts**, and each part performs a different job. Check them out on this diagram. And, after that, continue reading to learn about these electronic wonders that are **helping people around the world**.

1
SENSORS
These are the parts of a robot that allow it to gather information about its surroundings. For example, cameras gather images and microphones gather sound.

2
CONTROL SYSTEM
This is the robot's brain. It receives instructions from a computer and puts the commands into action.

3
DATA NETWORKS
This network is like the human nervous system. It shares information between the robot's control system and its other parts. Its components are housed in or on the robot's body.

This robot developed by NASA is called Valkyrie. It walks on two legs and has two hands, each with three fingers and a thumb.

The Five Main Parts of a Robot

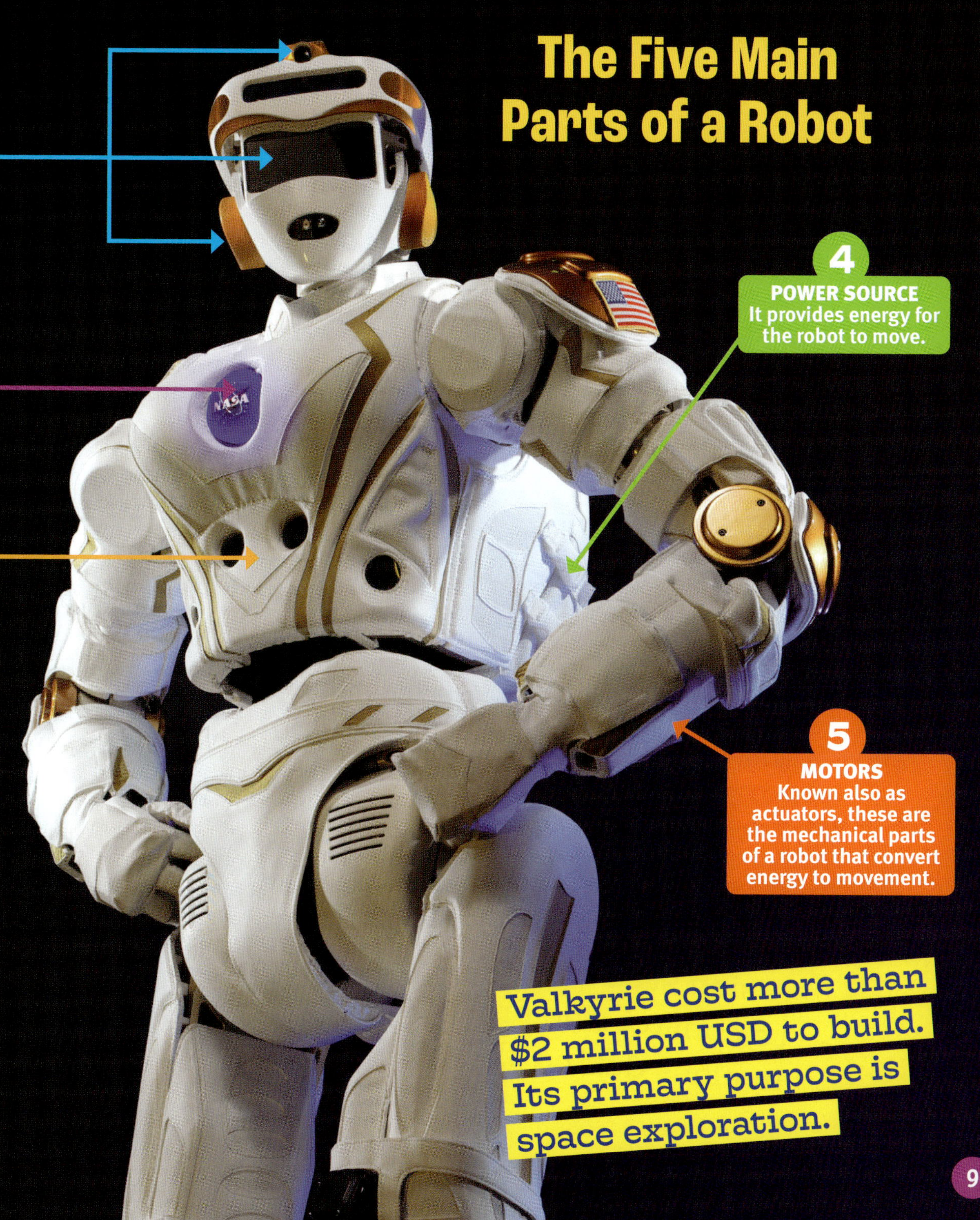

Valkyrie cost more than $2 million USD to build. Its primary purpose is space exploration.

Nao is a robot that goes to school for kids who are in the hospital.

A sick student can use a tablet to control Nao and participate in class during the school day.

CHAPTER

Everyday Robots

At one time, robots as we know them today were just characters in cartoons and science fiction stories. But **innovations** in robotic sensors, motors, and **artificial intelligence** (AI) made robots easier to build and cheaper to sell. Robots have been working in factories since the 1960s. More recently, robots have begun working in our homes—and even driving us around town. As technology improves, so will opportunities to put more robots to work.

Helping with Chores

Joe Jones first developed the Roomba in the 1990s. It could vacuum a floor by itself. It could also clean on a schedule. In 2002, the Roomba started vacuuming floors and carpets in homes, apartments, and offices. Not long after that, robotic brooms, mops, lawn mowers, pool cleaners, and window cleaners followed. Just charge them up and watch them go.

This robotic pool cleaner can roll right up the walls of a pool.

This robot can tell when strawberries are ready to be picked.

This robot can be seen delivering food on the streets of Los Angeles, California.

Robots Mean Business

Many robots are also used in business. They are trained to do a lot of repetitive tasks and heavy lifting. **Automated** cranes stack crates. Some robots move boxes in factories and warehouses. Others harvest strawberries. Hospital robots distribute medicines to patients. Robots deliver food and clean up spills in grocery stores.

The strongest robotic arm can lift objects that weigh as much as three adult cows.

Dr. Robot Is In

Surgery can be difficult and dangerous. Often, doctors must cut open their patients to help them get better. They must be very careful as they operate. This is where robots can help! Robots are very precise. They can work in tiny spaces. They can make surgery less dangerous. Doctors can do surgery with a robotic arm. First they make a small cut in a patient's body. Then they operate a robotic arm using a joystick and viewing screen. Patients can heal more quickly from the small cut.

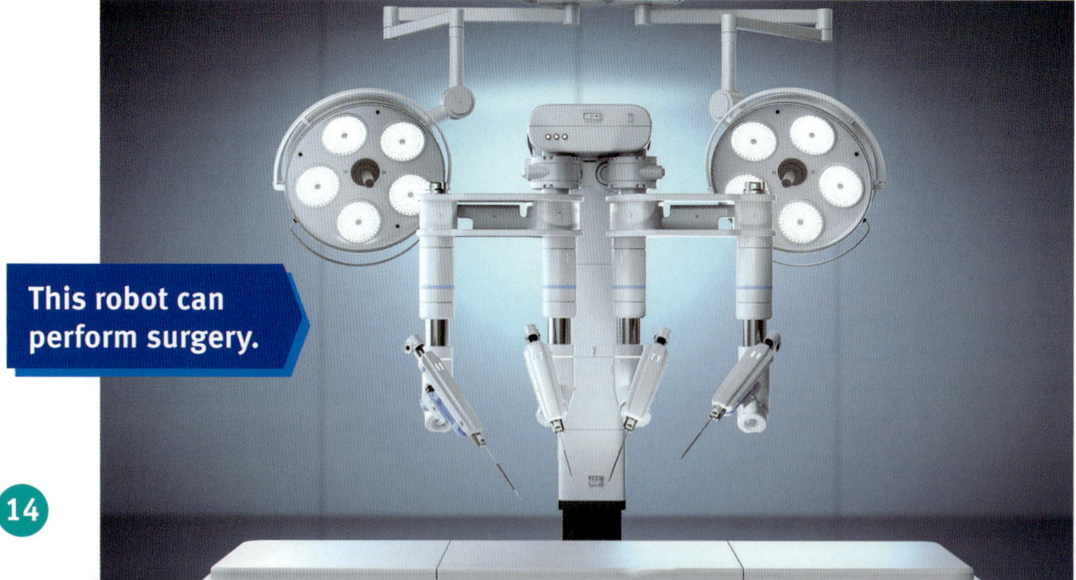

This robot can perform surgery.

The creators of RoboCup hope that robots will be advanced enough to compete against human soccer players by the year 2050.

RoboCup 2024 attracted 2,500 competitors from around 50 countries.

Friendly Games

There are also robots for fun and games. **Coders** worldwide have competed in RoboCup since the 1990s. They build teams of robots that play soccer, or fútbol, against one another. There are different leagues that feature different types of robots. There are tiny robot leagues, industrial robot leagues, and even rescue robot leagues. RoboCup organizers insist the games are a serious scientific project. They want to help coders build better robots.

Robot Friends?

Robots are machines. They do not have feelings like real friends do. However, scientists have created robots that can act like friends. They are called social robots. They can help support people when they need cheering up. There is even a robotic pet sitter that will watch, feed, and play with your pet while your family is on vacation.

Kirobo, shown here, is a robot friend that is able to recognize faces.

Fellow Human(oid)s

Robots are typically shaped to suit the work they perform. When it comes to robots that have to work alongside people, scientists think they should look a bit like us. That is why **humanoid** robots are built. They can use human tools and work alongside people. But building robots that can walk on two legs without falling over is hard and expensive. The same problem applies to teaching them how to act like humans. Scientists have not fully figured out how to solve these problems yet. However, AI is helping robots learn from their mistakes and adapt to their surroundings.

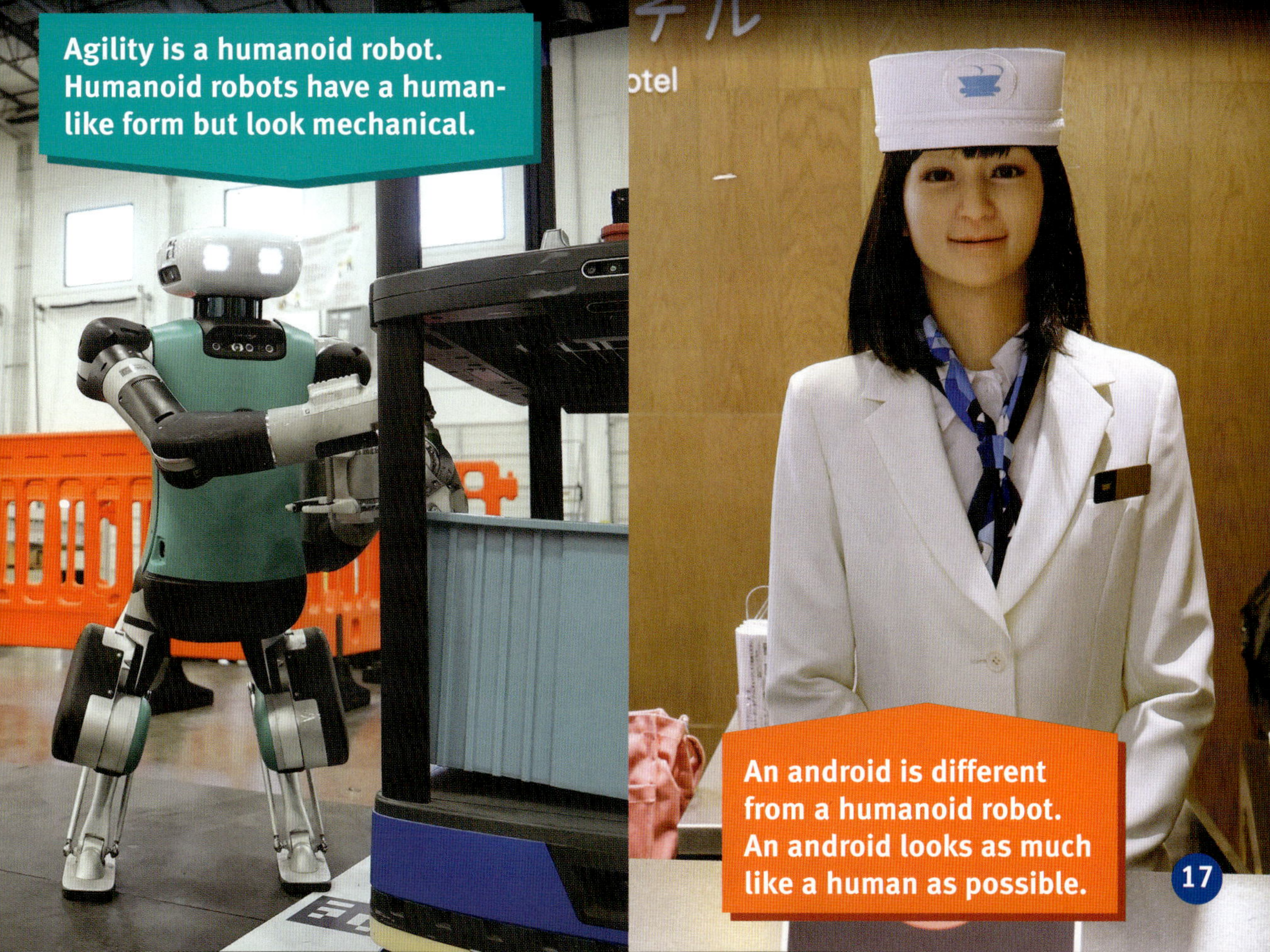

Agility is a humanoid robot. Humanoid robots have a human-like form but look mechanical.

An android is different from a humanoid robot. An android looks as much like a human as possible.

Unlike humans, Dante II can withstand hot steam and poisonous gases.

NASA's Dante II explores a volcano in Alaska.

CHAPTER

2

Exploring the Unknown

Some jobs are too dangerous for people to do—like crawling into a volcano. Some other jobs are still impossible for people to do—like visiting distant planets. Robots, on the other hand, can do just about anything. They can withstand extreme temperatures, extreme pressure, and more. They do not get sick, and they can last a long time. That is why, today, scientists are making robots that can handle some of the most dangerous and exciting jobs on Earth—and beyond.

Perseverance took a selfie on Mars.

In 2011, Robonaut 2 became the first humanoid robot in space. It returned to Earth in 2018 for repairs.

Space Missions

Robonaut 2 is a robot that worked on the International Space Station. Its graspers used the same tools astronauts use to do simple, repetitive, and dangerous tasks. Other robots that work in space do jobs that humans could not possibly do. Rover robots like *Curiosity* and *Perseverance* work on Mars—a planet that humans have yet to reach. The rovers collect images, environmental data, and samples. They also perform scientific experiments and send the data back to Earth.

Exploring the Deep

Scientists travel to the deepest parts of the ocean in specially made vehicles called submersibles. But the trip is expensive and dangerous. Pressure in the deepest ocean is equal to having 48 airplanes piled on top of you. That's where **autonomous** underwater vehicles (AUVs) come in. AUVs are robots that collect photos, videos, samples, and other important information about the ocean floor. The data helps scientists understand one of the least explored parts of our planet.

This is OceanOne, a robot that can explore the deep ocean. Scientists use a joystick to control it.

Making Risky Moves

No human would willingly crawl into an active volcano or swim under ice sheets. Instead, scientists send robots into volcanoes to better understand how they erupt. They also lower robots into dangerous gaps on an ice shelf. Data collected by these robots help scientists monitor how ice shelves are responding to **climate change**.

NASA's VolcanoBot can explore cracks in volcanoes that other robots can't reach.

A **drone** is a robot that flies. It can be used to explore volcanoes.

This robot is looking inside a hidden chamber in a pyramid.

Probing the Past

Some pyramids, like those in Egypt, have hidden chambers too narrow for humans to crawl through. A long time ago, explorers used dynamite to get inside—but that harms these historic structures. Now scientists have developed robots equipped with cameras that are small enough to fit in these narrow shafts without damaging them.

Small Wonders

Our bodies have parts so fragile that surgical tools could damage them. There are also parts these tools can't reach. Scientists have invented magnetic slime robots that can safely wiggle through our bodies. These "slimebots" can wrap around and retrieve accidentally swallowed objects. They can also move through openings to deliver medicine to hard-to-reach parts of the body.

This robot is made of magnetic slime.

Slimebots are also called soft robots.

Living Robots

In 2021, researchers created the world's first living robots. They took cells from African clawed frogs and **programmed** them to do certain tasks. They called the frog cells xenobots, after the frog's scientific name *Xenopus laevis*. The sand grain–sized xenobots can move microscopic objects. They use tiny, hair-like parts to move around. Researchers say they are good at collecting stuff. Someday, they hope xenobots can be used to clean the ocean of microplastics or help humans grow replacement organs.

Xenobots are an example of tiny robots called nanorobots, or nanobots.

This xenobot (inset) was made from an African clawed frog (above and right).

Some rescue robots, like the one shown here, work on land. Others work in water to rescue swimmers who are in trouble.

A rescue robot searches for survivors of an earthquake in China.

CHAPTER

3

Rolling Toward Danger

Firefighters, emergency medical technicians, and police officers are first responders. They have some of the most dangerous jobs in the world. So do the members of search and rescue teams—people who expose themselves to danger to save others when disaster strikes. Robots help these heroes get the job done. Though robots have not taken over these risky professions, they do help first responders and others work more safely and efficiently.

A firefighting robot blasts water at a fire.

Fighting Fires

When a burning building becomes too dangerous for people to enter, a firefighting robot is sent instead. Cameras and heat sensors on the robot help firefighters remotely lock onto the source of the fire. Then the robot blasts water on the fire to put it out. Drones can also help *prevent* fires. They drop “dragon eggs” to start small, controlled burns in forests. They burn dead branches that could fuel larger wildfires in the future.

Finding Survivors

After a disaster such as a hurricane or an earthquake, rescuers send in drones for a bird's-eye view of the area. That gives them information to plan a safe and fast route to survivors. Ground robots and snake-like robots can probe areas rescuers cannot fit into, like beneath the rubble after an earthquake. Sometimes, robots work as a team. Drones have short battery lives, so larger robots carry them close to the target area. Then the drones take flight.

This snake-like robot can be used to find people in collapsed buildings.

Robots in War Zones

Robots used in war zones can protect soldiers and civilians from harm. Military personnel control the robots from afar. Drones can scan remote areas. Ground robots can clear and disarm explosives. Robot rovers can move wounded people out of harm's way. But robots can also be used to launch remote attacks. Some people are worried that robots make fighting too impersonal and therefore more likely.

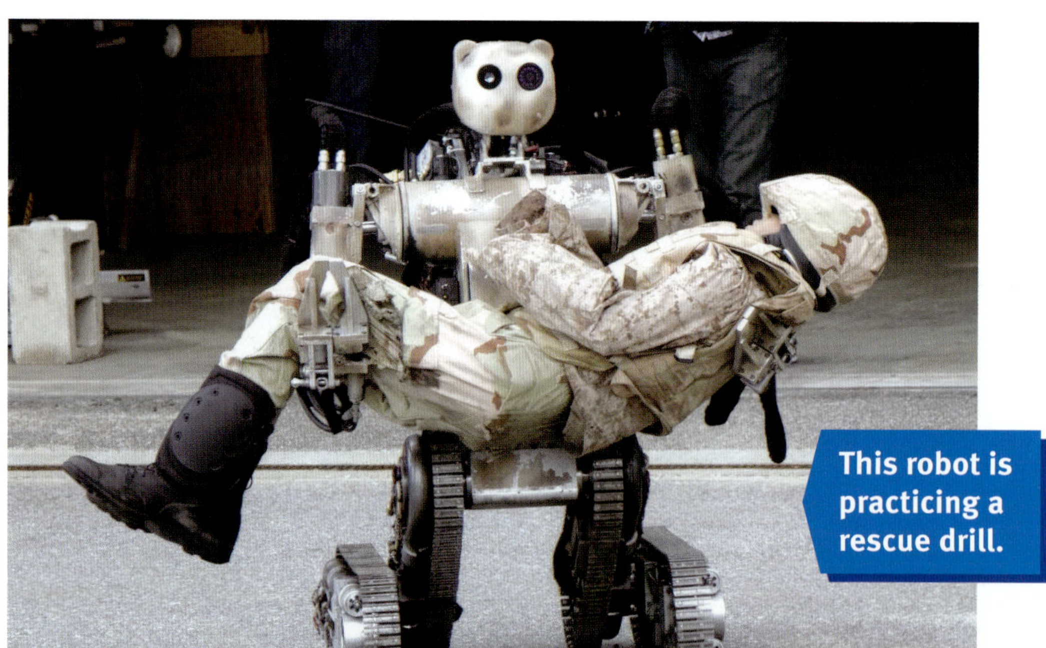

This robot is practicing a rescue drill.

This killer robot, or LAWS, carries grenades, which are small explosive devices.

In 2020, thousands of kids in Belgium voted to award a peace-keeping prize to the Campaign to Stop Killer Robots.

Banning Killer Robots

Lethal autonomous weapons systems (LAWS), also called killer robots, can use AI to decide when to fire weapons. Unlike many other robots used in combat, LAWS are not controlled by people. The United Nations is working on an international treaty to ban LAWS. Without a person making decisions, these robots could target and harm innocent people. Many human rights and religious organizations want them banned too.

Will Robots Take Our Jobs?

Some people are afraid of losing their jobs to robots. Could it happen? We cannot predict the future. But we can look at arguments from both sides.

NO

Robots cannot handle unpredictable events. Jobs often involve responding to unexpected events. Tremors can trap rescue robots. Sudden wind gusts can knock out drones. Power outages turn robots off. That is why robots need humans to make decisions in our complicated and unpredictable world.

Robots cannot solve complex problems. People can do different tasks, make decisions, learn from mistakes, and react to their environments. Robots can do only one or two specific tasks at a time, like lift crates all day.

Workplaces for robots are too expensive. Many workplaces are already built as safe places for people to work in. At this point, robots cannot just move into these places. Workplaces need to be designed and built around a robot's limited capabilities.

Robots are becoming more affordable.

Robots used to be expensive, so they were not used very much. But now they are getting cheaper to produce and sell.

Robots increase profits.

When a company uses one industrial robot, they do not need to pay salaries for six human workers.

YES

Robots are stronger and faster than humans.

Robots made of metal can lift heavier things than humans can. They do not get tired. They can keep doing the same task as fast as when they started.

More than four million robots worked in factories in 2023.

A robotic dog named HOUND holds the record for fastest 100 meters by a four-legged robot.

Meet BabyAlpha, a robotic dog introduced in 2023.

CHAPTER

4

Bio-Inspired Bots

A robot that behaves and looks like a plant or an animal is called a bio-inspired robot. Bio-inspired robots are designed to mimic behaviors and mechanical processes found in nature. They are helpful to humans in several ways. Sometimes they are companions to people who live alone or are suffering from health issues. In other cases, scientists make bio-inspired robots to solve problems. They want to understand how a plant's or an animal's special trait works and how it might be adapted to make the robot operate more effectively.

Way to Bee!

A lot of the food we eat comes from plants that have been pollinated by bees. And as with many pollinators, Earth's bee population has been decreasing. A robot bee that was developed in Europe can help the bees that remain. The robot dances in the same ways real bees do to show other bees where they can find food. Researchers are using the robot bees to steer real bees toward flowers that are free from harmful chemicals.

This RoboBee is about half the length of a paper clip.

Scientists used 108 videos of bee waggle dances to program RoboBee's dance.

Like a real bird, the smartbird (bottom) is a robot that flies by flapping its wings.

Imitating Nature

Researchers hope robots that are modeled after herring gulls will help engineers build energy-efficient drones and lightweight aircraft. Other robots are modeled after cuttlefish and marine flatworms that move using **undulating** fins. Researchers think the robots could help engineers build vehicles that can move on the sea floor without damaging coral reefs.

Mirumi is a furry little robot that clips onto your bag.

Robotic Pets

Robotic pets look just like real pets. But they do not have to be fed, bathed, or even walked. Robotic pets can be great for people who live in places where pets are not allowed. For example, the AlphaDog is popular in China, where, at one time, people were not allowed to have pet dogs. New York City has been giving senior citizens fuzzy robotic pups to help improve their quality of life.

Timeline: Robots in Modern History

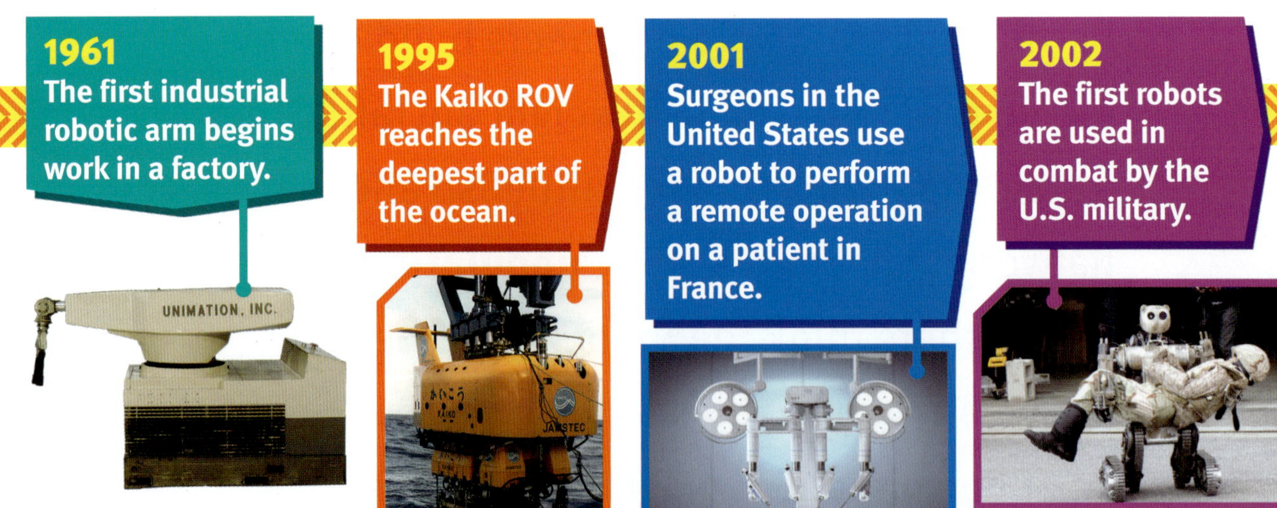

Robots of the Future

Robots extend our capabilities in amazing ways. And as they become more advanced, we may end up relying on robots more. Robots can help deliver medicine, food, and water to people in hard-to-reach places. New kinds of robots, like nanorobots, open up incredible possibilities in medicine. As researchers find ways for robots to better interact with humans and our environments, robots can support us in more ways in the future.

2011
Robots are the first to enter a damaged nuclear reactor in Japan.

2013
Kirobo keeps astronauts company on the International Space Station.

2024
Surgeons use nanorobots to perform surgery.

It Came from Hollywood

Many of today's robots seem to have come from fictional robots in movies and television. Here are four real-life robots and their likely fictional origins.

AERIAL VEHICLES OR UAVS

REAL LIFE

Also known as drones, these robots can fly and take aerial pictures and videos. They are often used for surveillance. Around 2016, civilians were given permission to fly them.

FICTION

The Jetsons (1960s)

One episode of this TV show featured a "snitcher picture taker." This robot caught one of the characters in the act when he sneaked out to watch a robot football game.

MOXIE

REAL LIFE

Moxie is a robotic friend for kids ages five to ten years old that was first introduced in 2020. The robot talks to kids about their feelings. It even helps improve kids' reading skills.

FICTION

Big Hero 6 (2014)

In this movie, robotics wiz Hiro Hamada is befriended by Baymax, an inflatable robot designed to take care of people.

ROBOTAXIS

REAL LIFE

These self-driving cars introduced in 2020 are hitting the streets in San Francisco and Phoenix in the United States, and Beijing and Shanghai in China. The driverless cars navigate using sensors, cameras, and software.

FICTION

The Adventures of Batman (1966)

On TV, Batman drove his car—called the Batmobile—when he was fighting crime. The Batmobile could also drive by itself or be remotely controlled.

NANOBOTS

REAL LIFE

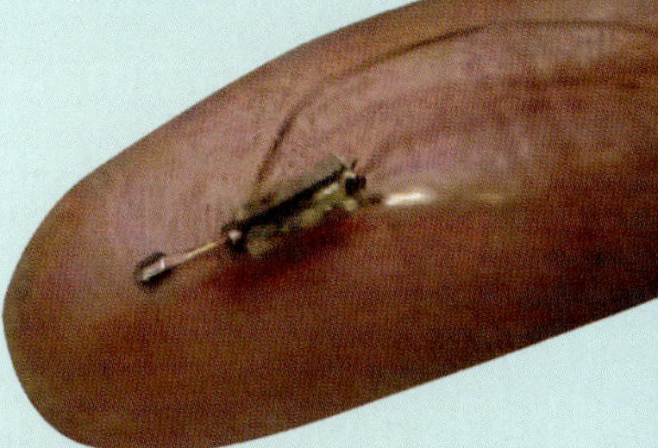

These tiny robots are injected into the body to detect diseases. Some can enter brain cells to find possible cancers and tumors. Nanobots that can enter the brain to treat burst blood vessels are also being developed.

FICTION

The Jetsons (1960s)

On one episode of *The Jetsons*, doctors used Peekaboo Prober Capsules. The tiny robots were used to explore inside a patient's body.

PERSONAL STORY:
From Coding to Robotics

Robots need step-by-step instructions to perform tasks, like moving, talking, or picking up things. These instructions are called codes. Writing code, or coding, is an important skill to learn as people live and work with more robots. You can join a robotics club, class, or camp where you will build a robot with teammates. You will learn how to write code and help one another teach the robot to perform different tasks.

Felicity Trujillo is a 13-year-old from Los Alamos, New Mexico. She is a citizen of the Chickasaw Nation. Felicity learned coding at a Sisterhood of Native American Coders (SONAC) camp with other kids. Read about her journey in robotics, which started with this coding camp!

I was in grade school when I attended the SONAC workshop. It was fun! I made new friends. I learned new coding techniques.

In one challenge, we needed to make something that would help the world in some way. My team wrote code for a "How are you feeling?" app for smartphones. If a kid clicks on "upset," for example, they get a message that helps them calm down.

After that, I learned more coding by myself. Then I learned more coding at a space and aviation camp at the NASA headquarters in Huntsville, Alabama. It was very exciting, and I got to work with my friends.

Thanks to my experiences, I became the captain of my school's robotics team. In 2023–2024 I was also the captain and driver of an intramural team called the Beta Hawks. We built and coded our own robot to complete a series of timed activities both autonomous and by a driver. We entered three robotics competitions in New Mexico and ranked second out of all the middle-school teams. The next year I served as the captain and first driver for the Alpha Hawks, another intramural team. We competed against middle-school and high-school teams from the United States and Mexico. Our team came in first in one of the tournaments!

Working with the team and competing against my peers was so much fun. I learned so much about robotics and coding—and about keeping cool under pressure!

True Statistics*

*As of 2024

- **Speed of the fastest two-legged running robot:** 9.06 miles per hour (14.58 kilometers per hour)
- **Lowest temperature endured by a two-legged robot:** -8°F (-22°C)
- **Highest temperature endured by a firefighting robot in France:** 1,652°F (900°C)
- **Pounds of pressure the AUV *Nereus* is built to withstand:** 15,000
- **Year that Flying Pigeon, the first robot, was made:** 400–300 BCE
- **Year of the first robot basketball competition:** 2012
- **Cost of the cheapest robot in the world:** $1.75 USD
- **Cost of the most expensive home robot in 2000:** $45,300 USD (TMSUK-4 is a robot assistant that stands four feet tall and was made in Japan.)
- **Number of factory robots in the world:** More than 4 million

Did you find the truth?

TRUE Scientists have sent robots inside volcanoes.

FALSE Robots cannot work in teams.

Resources

Other books in this series:

You can also look at:

Arnold, Nick. *Tools, Robotics and Gadgets Galore*. London: Welbeck Children's Books, 2018.

Gifford, Clive. *A Question of Technology: Will Robots Take Over the World?* London: Wayland, 2023.

Gifford, Clive. *Robographics: Super-smart Robots*. London: Hachette Children's Group, 2022.

Newland, Sonya. *Working with Computers and Robotics* (Kid Engineer). La Jolla, CA: Kane/Miller Book Publishers, 2022.

Glossary

artificial intelligence (ahr-tuh-FISH-uhl in-TEL-i-juhns) the science of making computers do things that previously needed human intelligence, such as understanding language

automated (AW-tuh-may-tuhd) operated by a machine

autonomous (aw-TAH-nuh-muhs) self-operating

climate change (KLYE-mit CHAYNJ) global warming and other changes in the weather and weather patterns that are happening because of human activity

coders (KOH-durz) people who write the instructions of a computer program

drone (DROHN) an aircraft without a pilot that is controlled remotely

humanoid (HYOO-muh-noyd) having a human form or characteristics

innovations (in-uh-VAY-shuhnz) new ideas or inventions

precision (pri-SIZH-uhn) the quality of being very careful or very accurate

programmed (PROH-gramd) gave a computer or other machine instructions to make it work in a certain way

toxic (TAHK-sik) poisonous, as in toxic waste

undulating (UHN-juh-lay-ting) moving in waves

Index

Page numbers in **bold** indicate illustrations.

About the Author

Natasha Vizcarra is a science journalist and children's book author based in Boulder, Colorado. She is originally from Quezon City, Philippines. Natasha loves cycling, gardening, and watching birds indoors with her cats. Visit her website at www.natashavizcarra.com.

Photos ©: back cover: Fang Dongxu/VCG/Getty Images; 3: © The RoboCup Federation; 4: The Robotics Institute/Carnegie Mellon University; 5 top: Embodied, Inc.; 5 bottom: frederic REGLAIN/Alamy Images; 6 top inset: JIM WILSON/The New York Times/Redux; 6 bottom inset: Peter Menzel/Science Source; 9: Bill Stafford/James Blair/Regan Geeseman/NASA/Wikimedia; 10–11: BSIP/UIG/Getty images; 12: Ethan Miller/Getty Images; 13 left: The Yomiuri Shimbun/AP Images; 14: PhonlamaiPhoto/Getty Images; 15: © The RoboCup Federation; 16: Kyodo/Newscom; 17 left: Agility Robotics; 17 right: frederic REGLAIN/Alamy Images; 18–19: The Robotics Institute/Carnegie Mellon University; 20: NASA/JPL-Caltech; 21: Osada/Seguin/DRASSM; 22: Ragnar Th Sigurdsson/ARCTIC IMAGES/Alamy Images; 23: Aladin Abdel Naby/Reuters/Redux; 24: Cover Images/ZUMAPRESS/Newscom; 25 main : piemags/nature/Alamy Images; 25 inset: Kriegman/Blackiston/Levin/Bongard/Wikimedia; 26–27: Imago/Xinhua/Alamy Images; 28: Kurita KAKU/Gamma-Rapho/Getty Images; 29: Kyodo/AP Images; 30: U.S. Army; 31: Scott Peterson/Getty Images; 34–35: Fang Dongxu/VCG/Getty Images; 36: Wyss Institute at Harvard University; 37: Festo AG & Co. KG.; 38 left: From the Collections of The Henry Ford. Gift of Unimation.; 38 center left: Kyodo News/Newscom; 38 center right: PhonlamaiPhoto/Getty Images; 38 right: U.S. Army; 39 left: AFLO/Newscom; 39 right: Kyodo/Newscom; 40 top left: Armyinform.com.ua/Wikimedia; 40 top right: Embodied, Inc.; 40 bottom right: Collection Christophel/Alamy Images; 41 top left: Dllu/Wikimedia; 41 top right: Copyright © 2012 Elsevier Inc. All rights reserved.; 41 bottom left: Greg Gard/Alamy Images; 41 bottom right: Wikimedia; 42 foreground, 43 inset: Courtesy Barbara Ryan; 44: Ragnar Th Sigurdsson/ARCTIC IMAGES/Alamy Images.

All other photos © Shutterstock.